THE ART OF NEGOTIATION

Unlock the Secrets to Successful Deal Making

Ray Goodwin

CONTENTS

LIABILITY DISCLAIMER

The information contained within this book is intended for informational purposes only and should not be construed as legal or professional advice. The authors and publishers of this book are not responsible for any losses or damages that may arise from the use of the information contained within.

The reader assumes full responsibility for any decisions made based on the information in this book. The authors and publishers do not endorse any particular method, service or product mentioned in this book and are not responsible for any consequences resulting from their use.

The reader should exercise caution and discretion when making life changing decisions, and should be aware of the risks and potential consequences of their actions. This book is not a substitute for professional or legal advice and should not be relied upon as such.

By reading and using the information in this book, the reader acknowledges and agrees to hold harmless the authors, publishers, and any other parties involved in the creation or distribution of this book from any and all liability, claims, damages, or losses that may arise from their use of the information contained herein.

CHAPTER 1: INTRODUCTION TO NEGOTIATION

Negotiation has always been an essential part of life, whether we realize it or not. From negotiating a salary with a potential employer to bargaining for the best price on goods and services, the ability to negotiate effectively can be the difference between success and failure. It's an art that can be learned and perfected over time. In this book, The Art of Negotiation, I will share my 25 years of experience in negotiating deals in various fields.

In this book, you will learn how to read people's body language, cues and understand what their true motives are. Knowing these skills will give you a distinct advantage in any negotiation scenario. We'll explore the different negotiation styles and strategies so that you can develop your own style based on your personality and communication preferences.

As we delve deeper into the art of negotiation, we'll examine the most common negotiation mistakes people make and provide practical tips on how to avoid them. Additionally, we'll cover ways to overcome common challenges such as difficult personalities or unexpected obstacles that may arise during a negotiation.

The ultimate goal of this book is to equip you with the necessary tools and techniques to become a master negotiator. Whether you're looking for better deals in business or everyday situations,

The Art of Negotiation is an essential guidebook for anyone who wants to improve their negotiation skills. So, let's get started!

Overview

Negotiation is a skill that we all use in our daily lives, whether we realize it or not. From small things like deciding where to eat with a friend to making big decisions such as investing in a business, negotiation is an inevitable part of our lives. In this chapter, we will explore what negotiation is, its different types, and its importance in our everyday lives. We will also look at the history of negotiation, its basic principles, and common misconceptions about negotiation.

Negotiation is defined as a process of communication between two or more parties with the aim of reaching a mutually beneficial agreement. Negotiation is a process that involves bargaining, persuasion, and compromise. It's important to understand that negotiation is not just about winning or getting what you want, but finding a solution that works for everyone involved.

Negotiation plays a critical role in our lives as it helps us navigate and resolve conflicts and disagreements. From personal relationships to business transactions, negotiation skills allow us to communicate effectively, manage conflict, and build relationships. Good negotiation skills also allow us to approach situations objectively, develop creative solutions, and understand other people's perspectives.

There are different types of negotiation, including distributive negotiation, integrative negotiation, and multiparty negotiation. Distributive negotiation is a win-lose approach where each party seeks to maximize their share of a fixed pie. This type of negotiation involves tactics such as making extreme first offers, making small concessions, and managing information to gain an advantage. Integrative negotiation, on the other hand, is a win-win approach where parties work towards creating value and finding mutually beneficial solutions. Multiparty negotiation involves more than two parties and can be particularly complex as the interests of each party may differ significantly.

Negotiation has a long history, dating back to ancient times. The ancient Greeks, Romans, and Chinese all had their techniques for negotiating. Over time, negotiation strategies and techniques have evolved, and today, we have a wealth of research and best practices to draw from.

It's common for people to have misconceptions about negotiation, such as believing that negotiation is only for business deals or that it's a zero-sum game. In reality, negotiation is an essential life skill that can be applied in a wide range of contexts, and it can lead to outcomes that benefit everyone involved.

The psychology of negotiation is also a vital component to understand. Emotions, biases, and personality traits can significantly impact the negotiation process. It's essential to consider the psychological aspects of negotiation and learn techniques to manage them effectively.

Culture plays a significant role in negotiation as well. Every culture has its unique values, beliefs, and attitudes, so it's important to be aware of these factors when negotiating with people from different cultural backgrounds. Failing to recognize these differences can lead to misunderstandings, misinterpretations, and negative outcomes.

In conclusion, the art of negotiation is a complex process that involves effective communication, planning, and creativity. The importance of negotiation cannot be overemphasized, as it is essential in our everyday lives, from small decisions to significant transactions. In the next chapter, we will explore how to prepare effectively for negotiations.

CHAPTER 2:
PREPARING FOR
NEGOTIATION

Negotiation is all about preparation; the more prepared you are, the more likely you are to achieve your goals. Successful negotiation requires a clear understanding of what you want, what the other party wants, and what the best possible outcome is. This chapter will cover the steps you should take to prepare for a negotiation and set yourself up for success.

Researching the other party

Before going into a negotiation, it's essential to research the other party. You need to understand their needs, strengths, weaknesses, values, and culture, to tailor your negotiation strategy accordingly. Look for information about their past negotiations, key decision-makers, and their priorities. Find out as much as you can about their business or organization, goals, products, services, and finances.

Defining and prioritizing goals

The next step is to define your goals and objectives. What do you want to achieve from this negotiation? Write down your goals and prioritize them in order of importance. This way, you can focus your efforts on what matters most to you and be clear on what you are willing to compromise on.

Identifying interests and needs

It's also essential to identify your interests and needs as well as the other party's interests and needs. Identify what motivates you and the other party to enter this negotiation. What are your underlying concerns, fears, and expectations? By understanding the interests and needs of both sides, you can see the bigger picture and find opportunities for mutual gains.

Anticipating challenges and obstacles

No negotiation is smooth sailing, and things can quickly go south if not handled correctly. Anticipate what challenges and obstacles you might face during the negotiation. What are the potential points of contention? Consider what leverage the other side has and think about how you can counter that. By anticipating challenges and obstacles and preparing for them, you can minimize their impact on the negotiation.

Creating strong opening positions

The opening position is crucial to the negotiation. It sets the tone for the rest of the negotiation and can influence the outcome. Your opening position should be clear, concise, and confident, and be backed up by facts and data. It should align with your goals and priorities and be realistic and reasonable. The other party will gauge your strength and commitment based on your opening position, so make sure it is well-crafted.

Setting limits and boundaries

Knowing your limits and boundaries is crucial in any negotiation. Identify your walk-away point, which is the point at which you are no longer willing to negotiate. This will safeguard you from making hasty decisions or conceding too much. Consider setting limits and boundaries for the other party as well and communicating these clearly during the negotiation.

Building rapport with the other party

Creating a positive rapport with the other party can help build trust and foster goodwill. Consider meeting with them before the negotiation to establish a relationship and find common ground. During the negotiation, focus on listening actively, building a dialogue, and showing respect for their viewpoints. Show your genuine interest in their concerns and needs and try to find areas of agreement.

Developing a negotiation strategy

Lastly, develop a negotiation strategy that incorporates all of the above steps and aligns with your goals. This strategy should be flexible and adaptable, as the negotiation may take unexpected turns along the way. You should also consider possible negotiation outcomes and how you will respond to these scenarios.

In conclusion, preparing for a negotiation requires careful planning, research, and preparation. It's essential to have a clear understanding of your goals, interests, limits, and priorities and the other party's as well. By anticipating potential challenges and obstacles and developing a clear negotiation strategy, you can set yourself up for a successful negotiation. Remember, the key to successful negotiation is preparation.

CHAPTER 3: COMMUNICATION SKILLS IN NEGOTIATION

Negotiating a successful agreement is heavily dependent on effective communication skills. This chapter explores the art of communication in negotiation and how it can lead to a better outcome for all parties involved.

Active Listening

Active listening is one of the most important communication skills in negotiation. It involves the ability to listen to and understand what the other party is saying, without interrupting or judging. Active listening can help in identifying the other party's concerns, interests, and needs, and it can help build mutual trust.

To practice active listening, a negotiator needs to demonstrate that they are fully engaged in the conversation. The negotiator can do this by asking open-ended questions and clarifying points that they do not understand. They should also reflect on what the other party said in their own words, to ensure that they have understood their message correctly. This will show the other party that their thoughts and ideas are valued.

Effective Questioning

Asking the right questions at the right time can lead to a better understanding of the other party's interests, needs, and concerns. Effective questioning is a crucial skill in negotiation, and it can help gather valuable information that can be used to create a more effective strategy.

Effective questioning involves asking open-ended questions that encourage the other party to explain their thoughts, ideas, and experiences further. This can help identify any underlying concerns, interests, or needs that may not have been stated initially. Effective questioning can also inspire the other party to think creatively and collaboratively about potential solutions to the negotiation.

Nonverbal Communication

Nonverbal communication is an essential negotiating skill that is often overlooked. It involves the use of body language, facial expressions, and gestures to convey messages that complement, contradict, or reinforce what is being said verbally. Neglecting to consider nonverbal communication can lead to misunderstandings and mistrust between the parties.

To improve nonverbal communication skills, a negotiator needs to pay attention to their own body language and that of the other party. They should maintain good eye contact, maintain an open and relaxed posture, and use appropriate gestures to convey their message. They should also be aware of the other party's nonverbal cues, such as facial expressions, tone of voice, and posture, which can indicate agreement, disagreement, or indifference.

Persuasive Language

The use of persuasive language in negotiation is an essential asset to any negotiator. It involves the ability to engage in an argument with an intention to influence the other party, and it can help the negotiator achieve their desired outcome.

To use persuasive language effectively, a negotiator needs to use language that is clear and concise. The negotiator should use language that resonates with the other party's interests, priorities, and concerns. They should be assertive in their language, making a strong case for their position, while remaining respectful and courteous to the other party.

Negotiation Jargon and Terminology

Negotiation jargon and terminology refer to the unique language used in negotiations. For successful negotiation, it is important for a negotiator to understand the jargon and terms used in their industry and the other party's industry, as this can help create clarity and understanding.

Clarity and Precision in Communication

Clear communication is essential in all negotiations. It involves the ability to express oneself effectively, using simple and concise language that is easy to understand. Using jargon and complicated language can lead to misunderstandings and confusion.

To ensure clarity and precision in communication, a negotiator should use simple language and avoid complex jargon whenever possible. They should also be specific and precise with their language, avoiding vague statements that may not convey a clear message.

Emotional Intelligence in Negotiation

Emotional intelligence involves the ability to recognize, understand, and manage one's own emotions and the emotions of others. In negotiation, emotional intelligence is essential, as emotions can have a significant impact on the outcome of the negotiation.

To develop emotional intelligence, a negotiator needs to be aware of their own emotions and recognize how they may be influencing their thinking and behavior. They should also be able to recognize and understand the emotions of the other party and adapt their communication style accordingly. They should remain calm and collected in difficult situations, using emotional intelligence to manage conflict and find mutually beneficial solutions.

Dealing with Difficult Personalities

Dealing with difficult personalities in a negotiation can be challenging, but it is essential to achieving a successful outcome. A negotiator may encounter people who are aggressive, passive, emotional, or analytical, and they should be able to adapt their communication style to effectively engage with these people.

To deal with difficult personalities, a negotiator needs to be adaptable in their communication style, recognizing that different people may require different approaches. They should also remain calm and collected in difficult situations, using emotional intelligence to manage conflict and find mutually beneficial solutions. Finally, a negotiator needs to be assertive in their language, communicating their position clearly and respectfully, while acknowledging the other party's concerns.

CHAPTER 4:
CREATING VALUE
IN NEGOTIATION

Negotiation is often portrayed as a conflict between two opposing parties working towards their own goals. While it is true that negotiations involve two parties working towards their own best interests, it is also important to remember the potential for collaboration and creating value during negotiations. By focusing on creating value, both parties can come out of the negotiation with a more positive outcome than if they had simply focused on getting what they wanted.

In this chapter, we will dive into the process of creating value in negotiation, including how to collaborate effectively, identify common ground, leverage differences, and build long-term relationships.

Understanding the Value Creation Process

The value creation process starts with identifying the needs and interests of both parties involved in the negotiation. This requires actively listening and asking questions to gain an understanding of what is most important to the other party. By doing so, both parties can identify potential areas for collaboration, leading to a more positive outcome for both sides.

Collaborating Effectively

Collaboration is a critical part of creating value in negotiation. This means working together to find a mutually beneficial solution. By sharing information and working towards a common goal, parties can increase the overall value of the outcome. Effective collaboration involves setting aside individual interests to focus on the greater good of the negotiation.

Brainstorming Solutions

Once the groundwork has been laid for collaborative efforts, parties can begin to brainstorm solutions to their identified needs and interests. This process should take into account the ideas and perspectives of both parties. By working together, the parties can sometimes find solutions that were not apparent when working alone.

Identifying Common Ground

Identifying common ground is an important part of creating value in negotiations. By identifying areas where both parties share similar desires or interests, it is possible to create a solution that meets both sides' needs. Identifying common ground is a win-win situation that can increase the likelihood of a positive outcome.

Creative Problem-Solving Techniques

In some cases, the identified needs and goals may not be easy to reconcile. In these scenarios, it is important to use creative problem-solving techniques to find a solution that works for both sides. This may involve thinking creatively to come up with innovative solutions or considering what compromises can be made to reach a mutually beneficial outcome.

Leveraging Differences and Diversity

Diverse perspectives can be a powerful tool in creating value in negotiation. By leveraging differences in culture, experience, and perspectives, parties can often come up with more comprehensive solutions. When working with parties from different cultures, it is important to consider and respect their cultural differences while looking for common ground.

Identifying Win-Win Outcomes

Once potential solutions have been identified, it is important to evaluate them with an eye towards creating a win-win outcome. This means finding a solution that meets the needs of both parties, increasing the overall value of the outcome as a result. Identifying a win-win outcome is a sign of effective value creation in negotiation.

Building Long-Term Relationships

Creating value in negotiation often involves building long-term relationships. By prioritizing a positive, collaborative negotiation process, parties can walk away from the negotiation with a greater sense of trust and respect for each other. This can lead to future opportunities for collaboration and an even more positive outcome in the future.

In summary, focusing on creating value in negotiation requires an open mind and a willingness to collaborate. By prioritizing the interests of both parties and working towards finding a mutually beneficial solution, both parties can walk away from the negotiation feeling satisfied with the outcome. This approach can lead to long-term relationships and opportunities for future collaboration.

CHAPTER 5: DEALING WITH CONFLICT IN NEGOTIATION

Negotiation is a process of communication between two or more parties with different interests to reach an agreement. The objective is to find a solution that satisfies everyone involved in the negotiation. However, sometimes negotiations become challenging, leading to conflicts that cause deadlocks in the process. Without an effective way to deal with conflicts, negotiations can derail and lead nowhere. In this chapter, we will address some strategies to mitigate conflicts in negotiations.

The Nature of Conflict in Negotiation

A conflict is a disagreement between two or more parties that need resolution. In a negotiation, conflict is a natural part of the process as parties have differing goals, interests, and opinions. Conflicts can arise from various sources such as:

❖ Differences in opinions on issues - parties may have different ideas about the desired outcome of the negotiation

❖ Competition - the parties may disagree on what they want, and both may see the situation as a zero-sum game

❖ Limited resources - when resources are limited, parties may fight over them

❖   Personality differences - the parties may not like, trust, or respect each other

These conflicts can lead to disputes and even disrupt the negotiation process, making it challenging to get an agreement.

The Five Conflict Styles

The five conflict styles are:

1. Accommodating: This style of conflict resolution involves prioritizing the relationship between the parties involved, even if it means sacrificing personal interests. An accommodator is more likely to accept a less than ideal outcome to maintain harmony.

2. Avoiding: This style of conflict resolution involves avoiding the conflict altogether, such as postponing the negotiation or moving the discussion to another venue.

3. Collaborating: This style of conflict resolution focuses on generating a win-win outcome, where both parties can get the best possible deal. A collaborator is more likely to creatively solve a problem by identifying common goals and means.

4. Competing: This style of conflict resolution involves focusing on a personal win, even if it means the other party has to lose. This style can be useful in situations where one party is seeking to establish power.

5. Compromising: This style of conflict resolution involves seeking an outcome where both parties give up something to get something in return. A compromiser is more likely to find a solution that satisfies both sides, even if the outcome is not the best possible.

Understanding and Managing Emotions

Emotions play a significant role in negotiating when the

stakes are high, and personalities are involved. People feel emotions differently, which makes it challenging to reconcile them. Resolving emotional conflicts requires acknowledging and addressing the emotions involved. Here are some strategies to effectively manage emotions in negotiation:

❖ Active Listening: Listening to what the other party is saying and how they are expressing their feelings is an effective strategy to manage emotions. It enables negotiators to understand the emotional content that underlies the disagreement.

❖ Empathy: Empathy involves stepping into the shoes of the other party to understand their emotions better. It helps to create a safe and respectful environment where both sides can express themselves freely and authentically.

❖ Addressing Emotions Directly: Addressing emotions directly is an effective way to manage them. It acknowledges that emotions are a legitimate part of the negotiation and the importance of acknowledging them to move forward.

Maintaining Objectivity and Professionalism

Negotiation is a process, and it is possible to become too emotionally invested in the desired outcome, leading to losing objectivity and professionalism. Maintaining objectivity and professionalism requires focusing on the negotiation problem rather than the person or group on the other side. The following are best practices to maintain objectivity and professionalism in negotiations:

❖ Establishing Ground Rules: Setting boundaries for acceptable conduct in the negotiation process will support maintaining objectivity and professionalism.

❖ Staying Calm and Focused: Staying calm and focused

can help negotiators deal with high-pressure situations and create a positive environment for constructive conflict resolution.

❖ Separating the Person from the Problem: It's essential to remember that the person on the other side is not the problem. Instead, it's important to focus on the issue at hand and the desired outcome.

Overcoming Impasse and Deadlock

Impasse and deadlock occur when the parties are unable to reach an agreement. These situations can be challenging to overcome in a negotiation. The following are strategies to overcome an impasse and deadlock:

❖ Find Common Ground: Identify the areas of agreement, as these can help in building a foundation for future negotiations.

❖ Identify the Underlying Interests: Identifying the underlying interests can reveal opportunities for creating value and developing a solution that meets the interests of both parties.

❖ Consider Alternatives: When the parties are at a deadlock, it's helpful to consider alternatives, such as looking for alternative sources for resources or expanding the available resources.

Using Third-Party Assistance

Sometimes, even the most skilled negotiators may not be able to resolve a conflict. In these cases, third-party assistance may prove helpful. Third-party assistance describes having a neutral third-party to facilitate the negotiation process. There are two types of third-party assistance:

❖ Mediation: The mediator works as a facilitator of the negotiation process, focusing on the interests of both parties and not taking sides. Mediators typically help summarize the discussion and point out areas of agreement and disagreement.

❖ Arbitration: In arbitration, parties submit the dispute to an independent third party who is authorized to make a binding decision.

Handling Unethical Behavior

During negotiations, unethical behavior can create conflicts and disrupt the negotiation process. It's important to identify and address unethical behavior effectively. Here are some best practices for handling unethical behavior in negotiations:

❖ Identify the Unethical Behavior: Recognizing and identifying unethical behavior is essential to addressing it effectively.

❖ Get Evidence: Obtaining clear and concise evidence of unethical behavior will help in addressing and correcting it.

❖ Address the Issue Immediately: Address the issue of unethical behavior as soon as possible to avoid the escalation of conflicts.

Handling Difficult Negotiations

Negotiations pose challenges that can make them difficult to manage. When facing difficult negotiations, the following are strategies to make the process easier:

❖ Prepare Adequately: Being well-prepared for negotiation sets the stage for the negotiation process. It's important to research and understand the goals, interests, and motivations of both side.

❖ Be Flexible: Being inflexible in negotiation prevents parties from reaching a mutually beneficial outcome. Being open and flexible to changing strategies and priorities can provide paths toward resolution.

❖ Stay Focused on the Goal: Keeping the desired outcome in focus, resolving the conflict, and moving forward will support moving past the difficult negotiation.

Conclusion

Conflict is a natural part of negotiation. With a grounded understanding of the different styles of conflict resolution, handling emotions, maintaining objectivity and professionalism, navigating impasse, and effective use of third-party assistance, successful negotiation is possible. Ultimately, successful negotiation is about acknowledging and managing conflict in ways that keep both parties walking away feeling as though they reached their goals.

CHAPTER 6: NEGOTIATING ACROSS CULTURES

In today's globalized world, negotiating across cultures is becoming increasingly common and important. Culture plays a significant role in influencing our behavior, beliefs, and values. Therefore, understanding and adapting to different cultural values and norms is essential for successful negotiation.

The impact of culture on negotiation:

Culture refers to a set of shared values, beliefs, norms, and customs that influence the way people interact with each other. Culture plays a crucial role in shaping our communication style, decision-making process, and behavior during negotiations. Understanding the impact of culture on negotiation is essential to avoid misunderstandings, build trust, and achieve positive outcomes.

Cultural values and norms:

Cultural values and norms influence the way people perceive and interpret information. They also inform how individuals prioritize and weigh different factors during negotiation. For instance, in some cultures, maintaining harmonious relationships and preserving face is more important than achieving individual goals. In contrast, in other cultures, individual success is prioritized over relational harmony. Negotiators from these cultures may have different approaches to negotiation, which may lead to misunderstandings, conflicts, or failed deals.

Understanding communication styles:

Effective communication is crucial for successful negotiation. However, communication styles may differ across cultures, which may lead to miscommunication and misunderstandings. For instance, in some cultures, direct communication is considered rude and confrontational, while in others, direct and explicit communication is preferred. It is essential to understand the communication style of the other party and adapt your communication style accordingly.

Perception and interpretation of time:

Time perception also varies across cultures and influences negotiation. Some cultures are punctual and perceive time as a scarce resource, while others are more relaxed about time and perceive it as a flexible resource. A negotiator from a culture that values punctuality may feel frustrated and disrespected if the other party is late for a meeting. In contrast, a negotiator from a culture that values flexibility may feel uncomfortable with strict deadlines. It is essential to understand the perception and interpretation of time in different cultures to manage expectations and avoid conflicts.

Building trust across cultures:

Trust is the foundation of successful negotiation. However, building trust across cultures may be challenging, as different cultures have different criteria for trustworthiness. In some cultures, trust is built through personal relationships and social connections, while in others, trust is built through expertise and professionalism. It is crucial to understand the criteria for trust in the other party's culture and demonstrate credibility and reliability accordingly.

Potential cultural misunderstandings:

Negotiating across cultures may lead to cultural misunderstandings, which may affect the negotiation process and outcome. For instance, in some cultures, a nodding head may signify agreement, while in others, it may signify listening or understanding. Similarly, the use of gestures, facial expressions, and tone of voice may have different meanings in different cultures. It is essential to be aware of these potential misunderstandings and clarify any unclear comments or actions during the negotiation.

Effective cross-cultural negotiation strategies:

To effectively negotiate across cultures, it is crucial to develop cross-cultural negotiation strategies. Here are some effective strategies:

- ❖ Conduct research about the other party's culture and prepare accordingly.

- ❖ Develop cross-cultural communication skills, including active listening, empathy, and adaptability.

- ❖ Find common ground and identify mutual interests.

- ❖ Focus on building relationships and establishing trust.

- ❖ Avoid making assumptions about the other party's behaviors or beliefs.

- ❖ Be patient and flexible during the negotiation process.

❖ Seek feedback and clarify any unclear comments or actions.

❖ Adapt your negotiation style to the other party's style while maintaining your assertiveness and integrity.

Adapting to different negotiation styles:

Negotiation styles may differ across cultures. For instance, negotiators from some cultures may start the negotiation with polite small talk and prefer a non-confrontational approach, while negotiators from other cultures may prefer a direct and firm approach. It is crucial to be aware of these differences and adapt your negotiation style accordingly, while remaining true to your values and goals.

In conclusion, negotiating across cultures requires an understanding of cultural values, norms, and communication styles. The effective adaptation to different cultures can lead to mutual benefits and successful deals. The development of cross-cultural negotiation strategies and the use of effective communication skills can help avoid misunderstandings and build trust, which can lead to positive outcomes for both parties.

CHAPTER 7: NEGOTIATING IN A BUSINESS CONTEXT

Negotiation is a fundamental part of business culture. From negotiating with suppliers and vendors to contract negotiations, businesses constantly engage in negotiation to achieve their desired goals. In this chapter, we will explore the different types of negotiations that take place in a business context and provide insights into how to handle challenging situations.

Negotiating with Suppliers and Vendors

Suppliers and vendors are vital partners to businesses. They provide the products, services, and materials that allow businesses to thrive. Negotiating with suppliers and vendors involves seeking favorable terms and conditions, such as pricing, delivery, and payment terms.

In negotiating with suppliers and vendors, it is essential to research the market and gain an understanding of the suppliers' and vendors' pricing policies. This knowledge can help in negotiating competitive rates that will satisfy both parties. It is also important to identify the key stakeholders within the supplier or vendor's organization and understand their interests, priorities, and decision-making processes. Building strong relationships with suppliers and vendors through regular communication and timely payment can also ensure smooth negotiations in the future.

Sales Negotiations

Sales negotiation is a critical aspect of any business that involves selling products or services. It involves persuading customers to agree to the terms and conditions of a sale, including the price, delivery, and payment terms. Sales negotiation aims to achieve a win-win outcome for both the business and the customer.

The key to successful sales negotiation is knowing the customer's needs and interests. Through active listening and effective questioning, businesses can gain an understanding of the customer's budget, preferences, and criteria, allowing them to tailor their offerings to meet these needs. It is also essential to articulate the value of the product or service and differentiate it from competitors. Building rapport with the customer and establishing trust can go a long way in securing a successful sales negotiation.

Mergers, Acquisitions, and Partnerships

Negotiating mergers, acquisitions, and partnerships involves complex negotiations that require a deep understanding of legal and financial matters. The stakes are high, and negotiations must be carefully managed to ensure that both parties maximize value while minimizing risk.

Effective negotiations in mergers, acquisitions, and partnerships involve understanding the key drivers for each party, including their vision, values, and goals. It is also important to engage experts, such as lawyers and accountants, to ensure that negotiations are grounded in sound legal and financial principles. Identifying synergies and developing creative solutions to complex issues can enable both parties to achieve their objectives.

Labor Negotiations

Negotiating with labor unions and employees is a critical aspect of managing a business. It involves bargaining for wages, benefits, working conditions, and other matters related to employees' employment.

Effective negotiations in labor relations require building strong relationships with employees and union representatives. Active listening and open communication can help in identifying key issues and solutions that will satisfy both parties. It is also crucial to have a clear understanding of relevant laws, regulations, and company policies. Creating incentives for meeting performance targets, such as productivity and profitability, can also encourage successful negotiations.

Negotiations in the Public Sector

Negotiating in the public sector involves issues related to government contracts, bids, and procurement. It involves engaging with government agencies and officials and requires a deep understanding of legal and regulatory frameworks.

Effective negotiations in the public sector require understanding the government's interests and priorities, including accountability, transparency, and service delivery. It is also essential to engage experts, such as lawyers and accountants, to ensure that negotiations are grounded in sound legal and financial principles. Building relationships with government officials, engaging in public consultations, and responding to the concerns and needs of stakeholders can facilitate successful negotiations.

Intellectual Property Negotiations

Intellectual property negotiations involve bargaining over rights and ownership of trademarks, patents, copyrights, and other forms of intellectual property. It involves negotiating agreements that protect the intellectual property owner's exclusive rights while allowing others to use the intellectual property under certain terms and conditions.

Effective negotiations in intellectual property require building strong relationships with stakeholders, including competitors, customers, and industry experts. Developing trust, engaging in open communication, and collaborating on mutually beneficial solutions can facilitate successful negotiations. It is also crucial to have a deep understanding of legal and regulatory frameworks, especially intellectual property laws.

Contract Negotiations

Contract negotiation is another important aspect of business that involves bargaining for terms and conditions that are mutually beneficial. It involves engaging with partners, contractors, and suppliers.

Effective negotiations in contract negotiations require identifying key issues and maintaining a deep understanding of relevant legal and regulatory frameworks. It is essential to build strong relationships with partners and suppliers through open communication, transparency, and prompt payment. Identifying win-win outcomes, such as shared benefits and cost savings, can also facilitate successful negotiations.

Handling Difficult Negotiations in Business

Negotiations can be difficult for several reasons, including conflicting interests, misunderstandings, cultural differences, and personal style. Handling difficult negotiations in business requires understanding the underlying issues and maintaining a strategic approach to achieve desired outcomes.

One effective approach to handling difficult negotiations in business is to seek the assistance of a mediator or neutral third party. Mediators can help parties identify common goals and interests and facilitate communication and understanding. Another approach is to use creative problem-solving techniques, such as brainstorming, to identify solutions that satisfy both parties' interests. It is also important to maintain open communication and remain committed to finding mutually beneficial solutions.

Conclusion

Negotiation is an essential part of business culture. It involves bargaining for terms and conditions that are mutually beneficial and represents a critical component of any business's success. Effective negotiation requires building strong relationships, understanding underlying issues, maintaining legal and regulatory frameworks, and adapting to cultural and personal differences. By understanding the nuances of negotiating in a business context, you can effectively manage relationships, achieve desired outcomes, and help your business thrive.

CHAPTER 8: NEGOTIATING IN A PERSONAL CONTEXT

Negotiation is not just reserved for the boardroom or business setting. It's a part of our daily lives, where we negotiate with family members, friends, service providers, and even strangers. Negotiating in our personal lives can be just as important as in our professional lives, if not more so. This chapter will explore some common personal situations where negotiation comes into play.

Negotiating in Personal Relationships

We negotiate with our partners, family, and friends all the time. Whether it is deciding where to go for dinner or how to split household responsibilities, negotiation is key to maintaining healthy relationships. The best way to ensure successful negotiations in personal relationships is to communicate openly and honestly. Make your needs and desires known, but also be willing to listen to the other person's perspective and needs. Be open to compromise and finding common ground, as this is key to maintaining positive relationships.

Buying or Selling a Home

The process of buying or selling a home is full of negotiations. From negotiating the price of the home to the terms of the contract, every step of the way involves some level of negotiation. When buying or selling a home, it's important to do your research and understand the current market conditions. This will help you to determine a fair asking price or make an informed offer. It is also advisable to have a real estate agent who has experience in negotiation as they can help you navigate the complexities of the transaction.

Negotiating with Service Providers

We often negotiate with service providers such as contractors, mechanics, or medical professionals. The key to successful negotiations with service providers is to establish a good rapport and relationship with them. This can be done by being courteous and respectful, and by communicating clearly and effectively. When negotiating with service providers, it's important to do your research, understand the scope of the work required, and have a clear budget in mind.

Negotiating Salary and Benefits

Negotiating salary and benefits can be a daunting task, but it's an important part of career development. Before entering into negotiations, it's important to research the market to understand the average salary for your position and industry. You should also consider your experience, qualifications, and achievements. Remember to negotiate for more than just salary – consider benefits such as health insurance, vacation time, and retirement plans.

Negotiating with Family Members

Negotiating with family members can be tricky, as emotions can often run high. However, the principles of negotiation still apply. When negotiating with family members, try to keep the discussion objective and avoid personal attacks. Listen to their perspective and identify areas where compromise is possible. It's also important to understand that not all negotiations will be successful, and it's okay to walk away from a negotiation that is not working.

Resolving Personal Disputes

Disputes can arise in any personal relationship, and it's important to address them quickly and fairly. When dealing with personal disputes, it's important to remain calm and rational. Listen to the other person's perspective and try to identify the underlying issues. Be willing to compromise or seek mediation if necessary. Remember that finding a resolution that is mutually beneficial is the ultimate goal.

Negotiating in Legal Situations

Negotiating in legal situations can be complex and stressful. Whether it's negotiating a divorce settlement or settling a personal injury case, it's important to have legal representation and to understand your rights and obligations. When negotiating with legal professionals, be clear about your objectives and priorities. Be willing to compromise, but also be aware of your bottom line. Keep in mind that reaching a settlement is often faster and less expensive than going to trial.

Negotiating in Community Settings

Community settings, such as homeowner associations or neighborhood groups, often require negotiations to resolve disputes or make decisions. The key to successful negotiations in community settings is to find common ground and establish clear objectives. Ensure that all parties are represented, and that decisions are made democratically and with the best interests of the community in mind.

In conclusion, negotiation is a part of our everyday lives. Learning how to negotiate effectively can help us in our personal and professional relationships. By following the principles of negotiation, communicating clearly and effectively, and being open to compromise, we can achieve mutually beneficial outcomes that enhance our lives and strengthen our relationships.

CHAPTER 9:
NEGOTIATING ONLINE

The advent of technology and the internet has brought about many changes in the way we do business and interact with others. The rise of online negotiation is one of the most significant changes, and it has affected various aspects of our lives. This chapter will explore the advantages and disadvantages of negotiating online, the challenges that come with it, and effective strategies to overcome those challenges.

Types of Online Negotiation Platforms

Online negotiation platforms come in different forms ranging from email, video conferencing, messaging apps, and collaborative platforms such as Google Docs and Trello. Each platform has unique features and benefits, and choosing the right platform for a particular negotiation depends on the nature of the negotiation and the parties involved.

Email is a popular platform for online negotiations because it is simple, reliable, and widely available. However, it is not suitable for complex negotiations or those that require real-time interaction. Video conferencing platforms such as Zoom, Skype, and Google Meet are excellent for face-to-face negotiation, just like in-person meetings, but they may not be suitable for negotiations that involve sensitive information due to security concerns. Instant messaging apps such as WhatsApp, Slack, and Telegram are great for quick interactions, but they may not be appropriate for extended negotiations.

Collaborative platforms such as Google Docs and Trello allow parties to collaborate on a document in real-time, which can be useful in complex negotiations. These platforms offer some advantages such as transparency, flexibility, and real-time collaboration, but they may not be suitable for negotiation involving sensitive information.

The Advantages and Disadvantages of Online Negotiation

Online negotiation has several advantages. First, it is convenient and saves time and money. Parties can negotiate from anywhere in the world at any time without the need for physical meetings. It eliminates the need for travel, which can be expensive and time-consuming. Online negotiation also allows parties to negotiate without being influenced by non-verbal cues or physical characteristics, which can affect the outcome of negotiations.

Online negotiation also offers some disadvantages, and one of the significant ones is the lack of face-to-face interaction, which can affect the level of trust between parties. Online communication can also be impersonal, easy to misinterpret, and prone to misunderstandings. Parties may also get distracted by other activities when negotiating online, making it challenging to focus on the negotiation.

Ensuring Privacy and Security in Online Negotiation

One of the most significant challenges of online negotiation is ensuring privacy and security. Parties must take extra measures to safeguard sensitive information that they share during the negotiation. Encryption is one strategy that parties can use to secure their communications. Platforms that use end-to-end encryption are more secure than others, and parties should choose those platforms for sensitive negotiations. Parties should also avoid sending sensitive information through unsecured channels such as email or social media.

Effective Communication in Online Negotiation

Effective communication is crucial in online negotiation. Parties must communicate clearly and concisely to avoid misunderstandings. Parties should avoid using technical jargon or terminology that the other party may not understand. Instead, they should use plain language and avoid unnecessary complexity. They should also be specific and precise in their communication, especially when agreeing on terms and conditions. Parties should also avoid using emoticons, abbreviations, and SMS language as they may be interpreted differently by the other party.

Building Trust in Online Negotiation

Building trust in online negotiation can be challenging, but it is essential for successful negotiation outcomes. Parties can build trust by being transparent, honest, and reliable. They should keep their promises and commitments and avoid making false promises. Parties should also disclose any relevant information that may affect the negotiation, even if it is not in their favor. Trust can also be built by maintaining regular communication and avoiding long periods of silence.

Overcoming Challenges in Online Negotiation

Online negotiation can be challenging, but parties can overcome those challenges by using effective negotiation strategies. One strategy is to establish ground rules for the negotiation, such as the mode of communication, expected response time, and types of information that can be shared. Parties should also aim to build a relationship with the other party before and during negotiation. Building rapport can help parties to understand each other's needs and interests, making it easier to find common ground. Parties should also prepare for the negotiation adequately by gathering relevant information and practicing the negotiation process.

Ethical Considerations in Online Negotiation

Ethical considerations in online negotiation are similar to those in face-to-face negotiation. Parties should avoid using unethical tactics such as lying, deceiving, or misrepresenting information to gain an advantage. They should also respect the other party's privacy and avoid disclosing confidential information without their consent. Parties should also ensure that they do not violate any laws or regulations when negotiating online.

Conclusion

Online negotiation is a significant development in the negotiation process, and it offers numerous advantages. However, it also comes with unique challenges that require careful planning and execution. Effective communication, building trust, and ensuring privacy and security are essential for successful negotiation outcomes. Parties should also be aware of the ethical considerations involved in online negotiation.

CHAPTER 10: INTERNATIONAL NEGOTIATION

In today's globalized world, international negotiation has become a vital skill for businesses, non-profits, and governments. It is essential to understand the unique complexities and challenges of international negotiation, including cultural differences, language barriers, and legal systems. International negotiations involve parties from different countries who bring their own cultural assumptions, communication styles, and perspectives. This chapter will cover some of the essential techniques and strategies for international negotiation.

The Influence of Culture in International Negotiation

Culture plays a significant role in international negotiations. Every country has its unique values, beliefs, and attitudes, which influence the way individuals approach business and negotiations. In some cultures, for example, indirect communication is more prevalent, while in others, direct communication is the norm. Additionally, opinions about time, relationships, and hierarchy vary widely in different cultures.

Managing Language Barriers

When conducting international negotiations, language barriers may arise, even if English is spoken as a common language. It is essential to be aware of the possible issues that could arise from these language differences. If the parties involved do not share the same language, interpreters may need to be present to translate the conversation in real-time. However, relying on interpreters poses a risk that ideas may become lost or misunderstood in translation. As such, it is imperative to use plain and straightforward language, avoiding colloquialisms and industry jargon.

Adapting to Different Legal Systems

Different countries also have their legal systems and regulations, and it's crucial to know the differences in laws, regulations, and legal practices before entering into negotiations. Differences in legal systems can lead to significantly varying approaches to negotiations, including the scope of what is negotiable and the level of power a negotiator has.

Dealing with Currency Exchange Rates

Negotiating internationally can also mean dealing with currency exchange rates. This can be daunting, but there are a variety of ways to approach this issue, including using a fixed currency such as the US dollar, hedging against currency fluctuations, or using an index-based exchange rate. Understanding how to cope with currency exchange rates is essential in ensuring that you are not losing money in the negotiation process.

Creating Effective Cross-border Partnerships

Before engaging in negotiation with people from different countries it is essential to research the parties involved to understand the unique cultural differences and communication styles that these parties may have. As previously mentioned, culture affects how people conduct business and how they negotiate. Unless these differences are appreciated and respected, negotiations may fail before they have even begun.

One important consideration in creating cross-border partnerships is to ensure that all contracts and other legal documentation are completed with support from those who are familiar with the local languages and customs. This helps businesses navigate the specific regulations and laws of different countries. It ensures that legal contracts are valid and is instantly recognized in both countries. In the long term, this also ensures that relationships between the negotiating parties can thrive and develop into mutually beneficial arrangements.

Managing Global Supply Chains

International negotiation deals with global supply chains, and negotiations generally involve both local and overseas suppliers. This requires effective communication and collaboration among parties with different cultural and linguistic backgrounds as well as operational structures. Establishing clear communication channels and agreeing on supply chain processes are essential to managing complex operating structures efficiently. Negotiation is essential in driving efficient production processes, encouraging collaboration, and ensuring smooth delivery. It is essential to manage supply chains effectively because any disruption could cause time delay in delivery, which could lead to significant reputational and financial impact.

Overcoming International Trade Disputes

Trade disputes are a common challenge in international negotiations. Global trade negotiators face complex disputes that require careful negotiations and tactfulness in finding solutions that address the challenges they face. The negotiation process in these situations requires innovative thinking, the ability to build relationships, and proficiency in dealing with the nuances of international law. In some instances, third-party negotiators may be brought in to resolve disputes. Seeking advice is essential in these instances, as it can help to manage conflicts to ensure all parties achieve mutually beneficial outcomes.

Conclusion

International negotiation is an essential skill in today's globalized world. It is essential to understand the unique challenges posed by cultural differences, language barriers, and legal systems, among other factors. To succeed in international negotiations, negotiating parties must respect and appreciate unique cultural differences, have effective communication skills, and learn how to adapt to different legal systems. Effective international negotiations ultimately result in successful partnerships, improved global supply chains, and increased competitive advantage.

CHAPTER 11: NEGOTIATING IN CRISIS SITUATIONS

Negotiation in a crisis situation is likely the most challenging and high-stakes type of negotiation one can encounter. Crisis negotiations involve situations where the parties involved are under emotional and physical stress, and decisions made during such negotiations can have far-reaching consequences. In such circumstances, it is essential to have a clear strategy and a calm head to ensure a mutually beneficial outcome.

The Nature of Crisis Negotiation

Crisis negotiations can take many forms, from hostage-taking to natural disasters. Crisis situations can be defined as sudden, unforeseen, and often dangerous events that threaten interests, values, and human life. The negotiations can either take place between two parties or involve multiple parties, such as in the case of a natural disaster. The stakes are high in such negotiations, as the decisions made can affect not just the parties involved but also the general public and even the wider global community.

Dealing with Hostile and Dangerous Situations

One of the hallmarks of a crisis negotiation is dealing with hostile and dangerous situations. The negotiating parties may be emotionally charged, and there may be a risk to life and property. The primary objective when negotiating in these situations is to diffuse the tension and create a safe environment for all involved.

Effective Communication in Crisis Negotiation

Effective communication is crucial during crisis negotiations. It is essential to establish a rapport with the other party and build trust. Active listening is critical, as it allows all parties to express their interests and needs. However, the communication should not just be verbal; non-verbal cues such as body language can also provide insight into the other party's feelings and intentions.

Managing Emotions and Stress

Negotiating in a crisis situation can be an incredibly stressful situation. The parties involved may be in a heightened emotional state, which can hinder the negotiation process. Effective stress management and coping mechanisms are necessary to help manage these heightened emotions. Emotions can quickly derail a negotiation, so remaining calm and professional is essential.

Responding to Terrorist Threats

The negotiation process in the case of a terrorist threat must be handled delicately. The primary concern is for the safety of those involved, and any negotiation should aim to achieve this. It is essential to remember that the motivation behind a terrorist threat is often political or ideological and not personal. It is also vital to remember that terrorists often resort to violence and threats because they believe it is their only means of achieving their objectives.

Handling Natural Disasters and Emergencies

Natural disasters and emergencies require an urgent response, and the negotiation process must reflect this urgency. The focus should be on protecting life and property and responding to the needs of those affected. In such situations, negotiations often take place between multiple parties in a collaborative effort to address the crisis.

Maintaining Ethical Standards in Crisis Negotiation

In a crisis situation, maintaining ethical standards can be difficult. The stress and urgency of the situation can lead to short-cuts being taken or ethical considerations being overlooked. However, ethical considerations are essential, and all negotiations should aim to achieve a mutually beneficial and ethical outcome.

Learning from Crisis Negotiation Experiences

Finally, it is important to evaluate and learn from crisis negotiation experiences continually. Experiences in a crisis situation can provide valuable insights into the effectiveness of particular strategies and techniques. These learnings can provide valuable input into future crisis negotiations and improve crisis response procedures.

Conclusion

Negotiating in a crisis situation can be incredibly stressful and challenging. However, it is essential to remain calm, professional, and ethical throughout the negotiation process. Effective communication, stress management, and rapport-building are critical in such situations. Understanding the unique challenges of crisis negotiation and developing a clear strategy can help achieve a successful and mutually beneficial outcome. It is essential to continuously learn and evaluate experiences in crisis negotiation, as this can help improve future crisis response procedures.

CHAPTER 12: POWER AND INFLUENCE IN NEGOTIATION

Negotiation is all about power. The more power one holds, the more leverage they have in negotiations. Conversely, the less powerful party is often forced to make concessions and settle on less favorable terms. Understanding power dynamics in negotiation can help one level the playing field and achieve better outcomes. In this chapter, we will discuss the sources of power, the role of status and reputation, and the importance of using ethical means to gain power and influence.

Sources of Power

Power in negotiation comes from various sources. Some sources of power are tangible, while others are not. The following are the main sources of power in negotiation:

❖ Coercive Power: This is the power to punish or threaten punishment. One who possesses this form of power can influence the other party to adhere to their demands by threatening punishment for non-compliance.

❖ Reward Power: This is the power to promise rewards for compliance. One who possesses this power can offer incentives or rewards to influence the other party to agree to their demands.

❖ Legitimate Power: This is the power that comes from the position one holds in an organization. Authority figures like managers, CEOs, and executives have this source of power, and they can use it to influence negotiations.

❖ Expert Power: This is the power that comes from having specialized knowledge or skills. Experts in their respective fields can leverage their expertise to gain an advantage in negotiations.

❖ Referent Power: This is the power that comes from admiration or respect. People who are highly respected or admired can use their status to influence the other party in a negotiation.

The Role of Status and Reputation

Status and reputation can also influence power dynamics in negotiation. Status refers to the relative position of a person in society, organization, or group. Reputation, on the other hand, is the public perception of a person's character, skills, or expertise. People with high status or reputation often have greater power as they can leverage their prestige and authority to influence the other party in a negotiation.

Building trust and credibility is a critical factor in establishing reputation and status. Trust and credibility can be built by demonstrating high ethical standards, providing value, being consistent and following through on commitments. People who are trustworthy and credible are often seen as reliable and respected, which gives them an advantage in negotiations.

Using Persuasion and Influence

Persuasion and influence are also critical in negotiation. Persuasion is the act of convincing someone to agree with one's position by using logic, evidence, and reason. Influence, on the other hand, is the ability to shape or change someone's behavior or beliefs. The following techniques can be used to influence the other party:

❖ Reciprocation: The act of exchanging benefits or favors can create a sense of obligation in the other party, increasing their willingness to compromise.

❖ Scarcity: Emphasizing the scarcity of a particular item or service can create a sense of urgency and increase the other party's motivation to agree.

❖ Authority: Citing experts or using a position of authority to support one's position can influence the other party's perception of the legitimacy of one's demands.

❖ Social Proof: Highlighting favorable experiences or reviews from others can create a sense of social proof, increasing the other party's willingness to accept one's terms.

❖ Liking: Building rapport and emphasizing similarities can increase the other party's liking and thus their willingness to agree.

The Ethics of Using Power and Influence

While power and influence can be effective in negotiation, it is essential to use them ethically. Unethical use of power and influence can cause long-term damage to one's reputation and credibility. One must consider the following ethical principles when using power and influence:

➢ Honesty: Being truthful about one's intentions and motivations.

➢ Respect: Respecting the other party's autonomy, choices, and dignity.

➢ Responsibility: Taking responsibility for the consequences of one's actions.

➢ Fairness: Ensuring fairness and equity in the negotiation process.

➢ Transparency: Being transparent about the negotiation process, one's position, and one's expectations.

➢ Compassion: Considering the other party's well-being and emotions.

Overcoming Power Imbalances

Negotiations usually involve power imbalances, with one party holding more power than the other. Overcoming power imbalances requires creative problem-solving and strategic thinking. One can overcome power imbalances by doing the following:

❖ Focusing on interests rather than positions.

❖ Creating opportunities to increase one's power.

❖ Building alliances and coalitions.

❖ Exploring alternative negotiation approaches like integrative negotiation rather than distributive negotiation.

❖ Building credibility and status through ethical behavior.

Empowering Others in Negotiation

Empowering others is critical in building long-term relationships and achieving sustainable outcomes in negotiation. Empowering others involves creating a sense of shared responsibility, setting clear expectations, and creating opportunities for feedback and participation. Empowering the other party can result in increased creativity, insights, and a sense of ownership and investment in the outcome. Empowering others can also create a more collaborative and cooperative negotiation process, resulting in better outcomes for all parties involved.

Conclusion

Power and influence play a critical role in negotiation. Understanding power dynamics and using power and influence ethically can help one level the playing field and achieve better outcomes. Building trust, credibility, and reputation can also help one gain power indirectly. Focusing on interests, creating shared responsibility, and empowering others can also contribute to achieving successful outcomes in negotiation.

CHAPTER 13: NEGOTIATION TECHNIQUES AND TACTICS

Negotiation tactics and techniques refer to the strategies employed by negotiators to reach a favorable outcome in a negotiation process. In this chapter, we will explore the different types of negotiation tactics and techniques and how you can use them to your advantage.

Basic Negotiation Techniques

- ❖ Establish a strong opening position: Your opening position should be strong, clear, and concise. You should state your goals and the expected outcome of the negotiation process.

- ❖ Active Listening: Listening is crucial in negotiation. To be an effective listener, you must be present in the moment and listen intently to what the other party is saying. When you are actively listening, you gain an understanding of the other party's needs and interests.

- ❖ Ask effective questions: To effectively communicate with the other party, you need to ask the right questions. Your questions should be open-ended, exploring questions that will guide the discussion toward mutually acceptable solutions.

❖ Persuasive language: The words you use have an impact on the negotiation process. Using persuasive language can help you influence the other party to see your point of view.

Negotiation Tactics

❖ Distributive Bargaining Tactics: This type of bargaining focuses on dividing up a fixed amount of resources. One party benefits from getting a better deal, while the other party suffers a loss. To be successful in distributive bargaining, you need to have a strong opening position and a clear understanding of your bottom line.

❖ Integrative Bargaining Tactics: This type of bargaining focuses on finding solutions that provide benefits to both parties. It seeks to expand the resources of the negotiation process so that both parties can benefit from the outcome.

❖ Persuasion Techniques: When used appropriately, persuasion techniques can help you achieve your negotiation goals. Some of the persuasion techniques include appealing to emotions, using social proof, and using scarcity.

❖ Anchoring and Framing: These techniques involve presenting the negotiation process in a certain way that positively impacts your position. You can anchor the discussion by presenting a high or low offer, giving the other party a starting point for the negotiation process.

❖ Concession Making and Trading: Concessions are an essential part of the negotiation process. It involves giving up something to get something in return. Successful negotiators know how to make concessions and trade them skillfully.

❖   Nibbling and Splitting the Difference: These techniques involve making small demands at the end of a negotiation to reduce the other party's resistance. By asking for small concessions, you can chip away at the other party's position, making it easier to achieve your goals.

❖   The Use of Silence and Pauses: Silence and pauses can be powerful negotiation tools. They can help you gain the upper hand in a negotiation process and make the other party feel uncomfortable. When used correctly, they can help you achieve your desired outcome.

Using negotiation tactics and techniques comes with ethical considerations. While some tactics can be useful, using unethical tactics can harm relationships, damage reputations, and lead to long-term negative effects. At all times, ensure that you are negotiating ethically and building relationships that are beneficial in the long run.

Conclusion

Negotiation is an art that requires skill and knowledge. To be successful, you need to understand the different types of negotiation and strategies that work in different negotiation situations. By using the negotiation tactics and techniques outlined in this chapter, you can achieve successful outcomes in your negotiations. Always remember to use ethical negotiation practices, avoid burning bridges, and focus on building long-term relationships.

CHAPTER 14: NEGOTIATING WITH DIFFERENT PERSONALITY TYPES

Negotiating with different personality types is a tricky task, but it's a necessary part of any successful negotiation. Understanding the different types of personalities can help you prepare for specific negotiation scenarios, adapt your negotiation style, and increase your chances of reaching mutually beneficial outcomes.

There are several different personality types that you may encounter during a negotiation. Here are some of the most common personality types and how to negotiate with them effectively:

1. Aggressive negotiators

Aggressive negotiators are often seen as tough, uncompromising, and confrontational. They tend to use strong language, make excessive demands, and use intimidating tactics to get their way. When dealing with an aggressive negotiator, it's essential to remain calm, stay focused on your objectives, and try to establish common ground. You may need to stand up for yourself but avoid getting into arguments or becoming defensive.

2. Passive negotiators

Passive negotiators tend to avoid confrontation and conflict at all costs. They may appear indecisive, uncertain, and easily swayed by others' opinions. If you're negotiating with a passive negotiator, it's essential to be patient, clear, and concise with your arguments. You may need to provide evidence to support your position, ask open-ended questions, and use active listening techniques to encourage them to speak up.

3. Emotional negotiators

Emotional negotiators tend to wear their hearts on their sleeves. They may become defensive, angry, or upset during negotiations if they feel that their interests or values are being disregarded. To negotiate with an emotional negotiator, it's essential to acknowledge their feelings, show empathy, and make sure they feel heard. You may need to pause the negotiations, let them vent their frustrations, or take a break to let them calm down.

4. Analytical negotiators

Analytical negotiators tend to be logical, data-driven, and detail-oriented. They may want to analyze every element of the negotiation before making any decisions, which can be time-consuming and frustrating for others. When negotiating with an analytical negotiator, it's essential to provide evidence to support your arguments, be prepared with your data, and anticipate objections. You may also need to speak their language, using facts, figures, or statistics to make your points.

5. Visionary negotiators

Visionary negotiators tend to focus on the big picture, thinking about the future and long-term possibilities. They may espouse big ideas, and their negotiating style may be more creative and flexible than others. To negotiate with a visionary negotiator, it's essential to share their enthusiasm, stay open to new ideas, and present your arguments as part of a larger, vision-driven agenda. You may also need to develop a relationship with them, as visionary negotiators tend to value the people they work with as much as the deal itself.

6. Multiple personalities

In some cases, you may find that you're negotiating with someone who exhibits different personality types depending on the situation. These changes can be tricky to navigate, as you may need to adapt your style depending on the moment. To negotiate with someone exhibiting multiple personalities, it's essential to remain calm, try to identify their preferences, and focus on building trust. You may also need to be adaptable, flexible, and willing to change your style to suit the situation.

Adapting your negotiation style to different personality types can be a challenge, but it's essential to remember that the goal is always to reach a mutually beneficial outcome. By identifying the other party's personality type, staying calm and focused, and remaining open to new ideas, you can build a relationship of trust and reach an agreement that satisfies both parties.

CHAPTER 15: MULTILATERAL NEGOTIATION

Negotiations that involve more than two parties are known as multilateral negotiations. These types of negotiations are often complex, and the dynamic is different from that of bilateral negotiations. Because there are multiple parties involved, it can be difficult to ensure that everyone's interests and needs are met. Therefore, it is essential to have a clear understanding of the multilateral negotiation process, the advantages, and disadvantages of this type of negotiation, and the techniques used to navigate complex negotiations effectively.

Understanding Multilateral Negotiation

Multilateral negotiation is a type of negotiation that involves three or more parties. In multilateral negotiations, it is essential to recognize that there is not just one other party to deal with; there are multiple parties with diverse interests and needs that must be considered. Each party brings their own goals and objectives to the table, and it is the job of the negotiator to find common ground between these parties and create an agreement that is acceptable to all involved.

The Advantages and Disadvantages of Multilateral Negotiation

The advantages of multilateral negotiations are numerous. First, multilateral negotiations can lead to more creative solutions to problems because multiple perspectives and ideas are brought to the table. Second, there is typically increased accountability in multilateral negotiations because everyone's interests must be considered and addressed. Third, individuals can leverage the power of the group to achieve their goals.

However, there are also disadvantages to multilateral negotiations. One major disadvantage is that negotiations can become bogged down with too many parties involved. In some cases, parties may also be less willing to compromise in front of other parties, which can make reaching an agreement more challenging. There is also an increased risk of confidentiality breaches in multilateral negotiations because there are more people involved who may leak critical information to others.

Techniques for Navigating Multilateral Negotiations

Navigating multilateral negotiations requires a particular set of skills and techniques. Here are some of the techniques that can be used to reach successful agreements:

1. Identify the Key Players

Multilateral negotiations can be confusing, so it's essential to know who the key players are. Identify the parties involved and learn as much about their interests and motivations as possible. Gain a thorough understanding of the negotiation's structure and add backup plans for when impasses are reached.

2. Continuously Communicate with All Parties Involved

Communication is a core part of any negotiation, but it is especially crucial in multilateral negotiations. All parties must have a clear understanding of each other's interests and needs, so everyone can work together towards a common goal. Miscommunication can lead to disagreements and derail the negotiation process completely.

3. Build Coalitions and Alliances

In multilateral negotiations, coalitions and alliances can be a powerful tool. Working with other parties who share similar interests and needs can help to achieve common goals.

4. Be Flexible and Open-minded

Flexibility is essential in multilateral negotiations. Individuals must remain open to changing their position or approach to achieve the overall goal. In some cases, splitting the difference or finding a creative solution that meets everyone's needs may be necessary.

5. Keep the Negotiation Focused

Keeping all parties focused on finding solutions is critical in multilateral negotiations. Often in multilateral negotiations, parties may want to delve into their individual grievances. But negotiating parties must remain focused on the end goals and avoiding deadlock.

6. Understand the Cultural Differences

Cultural differences play a significant role in multilateral negotiations, and it is essential to understand them and how they influence perspectives and decision-making. Cultural differences may affect communication and decision-making styles and must be navigated to reach successful agreements.

7. Bring in an Impartial Mediator

In some multilateral negotiations, it may be necessary to bring in an impartial mediator to help manage the negotiation process, especially if the negotiation is becoming too contentious. A mediator can help bridge divided perspectives and meet common needs.

Conclusion

Multilateral negotiations can provide substantial benefits compared to bilateral negotiations; however, they can also be more difficult to manage. Being aware of the challenges of multilateral negotiations and the techniques to navigate them effectively can lead to better results and stronger relationships among parties. Ultimately, it is essential to remain focused on the key issues and remain open to creative solutions to meet everyone's needs.

CHAPTER 16: ETHICS IN NEGOTIATION

When we think about negotiation, we often focus on achieving our goals and getting what we want. However, negotiation is not just about winning - it's about finding a mutually beneficial agreement that meets the needs of all parties involved. This is where ethics come into play. Ethical negotiation practices are crucial for building trust, maintaining relationships, and ensuring long-term success. In this chapter, we will explore the importance of ethical behavior in negotiation and provide strategies for making ethical decisions.

Understanding ethical principles in negotiation

Ethics are moral principles that govern behavior. In negotiation, ethical principles are the values and standards that guide our conduct. The most important ethical principles in negotiation are honesty, integrity, fairness, and respect. These principles can be traced back to the golden rule - treating others as you would like to be treated.

Honesty is the cornerstone of ethical behavior in negotiation. It's important to be truthful and transparent about your goals, interests, and needs. This means avoiding deception, half-truths, and lies. If you are caught in a lie, you will lose credibility and trust. Once trust is lost, it's difficult to regain.

Integrity is the quality of being honest and having strong moral principles. It's important to stand by your word and honor commitments. When you make a promise, you need to keep it. Even if it's not the best outcome for you, it's important to act with integrity and do what's right.

Fairness means treating all parties equally and striving for a win-win outcome. This means avoiding aggressive tactics that result in an unfair advantage. Negotiation is not a zero-sum game - there is usually a solution that meets the needs of all parties. It's important to be open-minded and listen to the needs of the other party.

Respect means treating others with dignity and acknowledging their needs. It's important to recognize that people have different perspectives, priorities, and values. By showing respect, you build trust and create a positive negotiating environment.

The impact of unethical behavior in negotiation

Unethical behavior can have serious consequences in negotiation. If you engage in unethical behavior, you risk damaging relationships, losing credibility, and facing legal or financial repercussions. Furthermore, unethical behavior can create a negative reputation that can follow you throughout your career.

Dishonesty, for example, can lead to broken deals, lost partnerships, and a tarnished reputation. By contrast, honesty builds trust, encourages transparency, and leads to long-lasting relationships. Similarly, aggressive tactics can lead to a win-lose outcome, destroying the possibility of a mutually-beneficial agreement. By fostering a collaborative and respectful negotiation environment, ethical negotiators can create positive outcomes that benefit all parties involved.

Common ethical dilemmas in negotiation

Ethical dilemmas can arise in negotiation when different ethical principles conflict with one another. Below are a few ethical dilemmas that commonly arise in negotiation:

❖ Confidentiality vs. Honesty - In some cases, confidentiality agreements prevent negotiators from sharing important information with the other party. However, withholding information can be viewed as dishonest and violates trust.

❖ Transparency vs. Privacy - In some cases, sharing too much information can put a negotiator at a disadvantage. Conversely, withholding information can be seen as unethical. Finding a balance between transparency and privacy is crucial.

❖ Fairness vs. Competitive Advantage - Aggressive tactics can provide a competitive advantage in negotiation. However, they can also violate the principle of fairness. Negotiators must balance the need for a competitive advantage with the principle of fairness.

Balancing honesty and transparency with confidentiality

Honesty and transparency are crucial for building trust and maintaining ethical standards in negotiation. At the same time, confidentiality is often required to protect sensitive information. Negotiators must balance these two principles to find a solution that meets the needs of all parties. Below are a few strategies for balancing honesty and transparency with confidentiality:

❖ Only share confidential information when necessary. In some cases, it may be possible to redact sensitive information or provide summaries instead of full documents.

❖ Be upfront about what information can be shared and what cannot. Setting expectations upfront can prevent misunderstandings in the negotiation process.

❖ Consider using a third-party mediator to facilitate communication. Mediators can be a neutral party that helps both sides navigate the negotiation process while maintaining confidentiality.

The role of trust and credibility in ethical negotiation

Trust and credibility are fundamental to ethical behavior in negotiation. Without trust, agreements cannot be reached, and relationships cannot be maintained. Trust is built through a consistent demonstration of ethical behavior. To build trust, it's crucial to:

❖ Be honest and transparent

❖ Follow through on commitments

❖ Listen actively

❖ Demonstrate respect

❖ Maintain confidentiality

❖ Apologize for mistakes

The more trust you build, the more likely it is that you will be able to develop successful negotiation outcomes and navigate any conflict that may arise.

Ethical considerations in distributive bargaining

Distributive bargaining is a negotiation approach where the parties compete for a fixed pie of resources. Distributive bargaining can create ethical challenges, especially if the parties have unequal bargaining power. Below are a few ethical considerations to keep in mind when engaging in distributive bargaining:

❖ Avoid deception or misleading tactics

❖ Consider what is fair and equitable

❖ Be transparent about your needs and interests

❖ Strive for a mutually beneficial agreement

❖ Ensure that the outcome is not harmful to either party

❖ Ensuring fairness and equity in negotiation

Fairness is a fundamental ethical principle that guides behavior in negotiation. To ensure a fair negotiation outcome, negotiators must:

❖ Avoid aggressive tactics that put one party at a disadvantage

❖ Listen to the needs of both parties

❖ Consider what is fair and equitable

❖ Strive for a win-win result

❖ Maintain transparency and honesty

❖ Be respectful

Learning from ethical negotiation experiences

Negotiation is a learning process. Even ethical negotiators can make mistakes. To learn from ethical negotiation experiences, consider:

❖ Reflecting on the negotiation process

❖ Identifying what you did wrong

❖ Understanding why it was wrong

❖ Creating a plan for how to avoid similar mistakes in the future

❖ Asking for feedback from the other party

Conclusion

Negotiation is not just about getting what you want, it's about building relationships and finding mutually beneficial solutions. Ethical behavior is crucial for achieving success in negotiation. By following ethical principles and building trust, negotiators can create positive outcomes that benefit all parties involved. By truly engaging in ethical negotiation, we can create a world that is equitable, respectful, and just.

CHAPTER 17:
NEGOTIATION AND
DECISION MAKING

Negotiation is not just about reaching an agreement between two parties: it's also about making decisions. In fact, every negotiation involves some level of decision-making. As such, understanding the decision-making process and how it relates to negotiation is crucial for negotiators.

The Decision-Making Process:

Decision-making involves selecting one option among several alternatives with the goal of achieving a desired outcome. The decision-making process often consists of the following stages:

- ❖ Identifying the problem or opportunity: This involves recognizing the need to make a decision and identifying the specific issue that needs to be addressed.

- ❖ Gathering information: This involves collecting information on the options available and evaluating the potential outcomes of each option.

- ❖ Evaluating alternatives: This involves assessing the pros and cons of each available option.

- ❖ Selecting the best alternative: Based on the evaluation of each alternative, the best option is chosen.

❖ Implementing the decision: The chosen option is put into action.

❖ Evaluating the decision: The outcome of the decision is assessed to determine whether the desired outcome was achieved.

Negotiation and Decision Making:

Negotiators face several challenges when making decisions in the negotiation process. These can include biases, emotions, and limited information.

Cognitive Biases:

Cognitive biases are errors in thinking that can affect decision-making. Negotiators should be aware of these biases to avoid making irrational or sub-optimal decisions.

One common bias is the Anchoring Bias, where negotiators unfairly focus on the first piece of information presented to them. For example, an initial offer in a negotiation can heavily influence the final outcome.

The Confirmation Bias is another bias that causes negotiators to seek out information that confirms their current beliefs or preconceptions. This bias can result in negotiators being blind to other options that may be better suited to their needs.

Emotions:

Emotions can influence decision-making in the negotiation process. Emotions can cause negotiators to overvalue or undervalue certain aspects of the negotiation, leading to suboptimal decisions.

One useful strategy in managing emotions is to take a break. By stepping away from the negotiation table, negotiators can gain some distance from the emotions and refocus on the decision at hand.

Limited Information:

Negotiators often face situations where they lack sufficient information to make an informed decision. In these cases, they may need to use estimates or assumptions to move forward.

One approach to dealing with limited information is to conduct a thorough analysis of available information and generate a range of possible scenarios. This can help negotiators identify potential risks and opportunities.

Decision-Making Tools and Techniques:

There are various decision-making tools and techniques available to negotiators. One example is the Decision Matrix, which involves creating a table to evaluate different options against pre-defined criteria. This can help negotiators systematically evaluate alternatives in a structured way.

Another tool is SWOT Analysis, which stands for Strengths, Weaknesses, Opportunities, and Threats. This technique involves evaluating the internal strengths and weaknesses of a decision, along with external opportunities and threats.

Ethics of Decision Making in Negotiation:

In negotiations, ethical considerations must also be taken into account when making decisions. Negotiators should consider issues such as fairness, honesty, and transparency when evaluating alternatives.

Negotiators should also consider the impact of their decisions on other stakeholders and society as a whole. Decisions made in negotiations can have significant impacts and must be weighed carefully.

Learning from Decision-Making Experiences:

Negotiators should also reflect on their experiences with decision-making in negotiations. By reflecting on past decisions, negotiators can identify what worked well and what did not.

Negotiators should also seek feedback from others involved in the negotiation process. This can help them understand how their decisions impacted others and identify areas for improvement.

In conclusion, negotiation and decision-making are intricately linked. Negotiators must be aware of biases, emotions, and limited information when making decisions in negotiations. Using decision-making tools and approaches can help negotiators make informed decisions. Finally, negotiators must consider ethical considerations and seek to learn from past decision-making experiences.

CHAPTER 18:
NEGOTIATION
AND EMOTION

Negotiation is a process that involves emotion. Whether we like it or not, emotions will always play a significant role in any negotiation. Emotions can contribute positively or negatively to the negotiation process, and if not managed properly, they can lead to a breakdown in communication or a failed negotiation.

The Role of Emotion in Negotiation

Emotions are an essential element in negotiation for various reasons. First, emotions are an indication of how vital the negotiation is to the parties involved. If people are not emotionally invested, they will not care about the outcome or put in the effort required to reach an agreement. Additionally, feelings reflect the parties' beliefs, values, and needs, which can influence the negotiation's dynamic.

Emotions can also serve as a tool for persuasion in negotiation. During a negotiation, people may use emotions to convince others to agree with their position. For example, expressing disappointment or frustration may lead the other party to change their position to avoid upsetting the other person. Emotional appeals can also work in reverse, with negotiators playing on the other party's emotions to achieve their desired outcome.

The Impact of Emotion on Decision Making

Emotions can significantly influence decision-making in negotiation. People typically make decisions driven by their emotions rather than logic. During a negotiation, emotions can influence the decision-making process in several ways. For example, negotiators' emotions can prevent them from seeing the other party's perspective or bias their view of the situation.

Negotiators' emotional responses can also result in irrational and regretful decisions. For example, a person may agree to a bad deal because they feel pressured or fearful of the consequences of not reaching an agreement. Conversely, a negotiator may walk away from a good deal due to frustration or anger with the process or the other party.

Managing Emotions in Negotiation

Since emotions play such a significant role in negotiation, managing emotional responses is essential for successful negotiations. Below are some strategies that negotiators can use to manage their emotions during a negotiation:

1. Recognize your emotions

The first step in managing emotions during a negotiation is awareness. Recognizing your emotional responses can help you manage them better. Being aware of the emotions that you and the other party are feeling allows you to keep the conversation on track and avoid any emotional outbursts or irrational decisions.

2. Review your triggers

Gaining an understanding of what triggers your emotional responses during negotiation can help you manage your reactions better. Reflecting on past negotiations and identifying the specific emotions you experienced can help you prepare for future negotiations.

3. Develop emotional intelligence

Emotional intelligence is the ability to recognize and manage your feelings and emotions as well as others'. Developing emotional intelligence allows you to recognize what the other party is feeling and respond effectively. By understanding the other party's emotions and feelings, you can tailor your communication to reduce friction and achieve a desirable outcome.

4. Plan for success

Planning and preparing for a negotiation can help you manage your emotions better. By developing a negotiation plan, you can outline your goals, identify potential pitfalls, and establish your ideal negotiation outcome. By having a clear plan, you can focus your attention on achieving your goals and setting achievable expectations.

5. Maintain composure

Maintaining composure during a negotiation is crucial for successful outcomes. Staying calm and composed, especially when tempers flare or the conversation becomes heated, can lead to more productive discussions and better negotiation results.

6. Incorporate breaks

Negotiations can be tense and emotionally draining. Incorporating breaks in your negotiation plan can help manage your emotions by providing time to recharge and de-escalate when tensions run high. Breaks can also give you time to reflect on the negotiation and refocus your attention on the end goal.

Conclusion

Emotions play an integral role in negotiation, and their impact should not be underestimated. By recognizing the role of emotions and managing emotional responses effectively, negotiators can create more productive outcomes that benefit all parties involved. By incorporating emotional intelligence, planning for success, and maintaining composure, negotiators can negotiate more effectively and create better working relationships. Understanding the emotional aspect of negotiation is fundamental to mastering the art of negotiation.

CHAPTER 19:
NEGOTIATION AND
LEADERSHIP

Negotiation and leadership go hand in hand, as effective leaders must be able to negotiate skilfully to achieve their goals. Whether in business, government, or any other field, leaders need to negotiate with stakeholders, collaborators, and competitors to make decisions, allocate resources, and solve problems. In this chapter, we will explore the relationship between negotiation and leadership, identify leadership styles and negotiation strategies, and discuss ways to overcome leadership challenges in negotiation.

Leadership Styles in Negotiation

Leadership styles can have a significant impact on negotiation outcomes, as they shape how leaders interact with others and make decisions. Here are some common leadership styles and their implications for negotiation:

❖   Authoritarian: Authoritarian leaders make decisions without consulting others and use their power to enforce their will. In negotiation, this style can be effective when dealing with subordinates or in crisis situations, but it can also create resistance and mistrust, among others.

❖ Democratic: Democratic leaders engage others in decision making and delegate authority to them. In negotiation, this style can be effective for building consensus and trust, but it can also slow down the process and lead to gridlock.

❖ Transformational: Transformational leaders inspire and motivate others to work towards a shared vision. In negotiation, this style can be effective for building long-term relationships and creating win-win outcomes, but it may require more time and effort to develop.

❖ Transactional: Transactional leaders reward or punish others based on their performance. In negotiation, this style can be effective for achieving short-term goals and enforcing agreements, but it may not foster creativity or collaboration.

❖ Servant: Servant leaders prioritize the needs of others and use their power to serve them. In negotiation, this style can be effective for building trust and rapport, but it may require more compromise and flexibility than other styles.

Effective Negotiation Strategies for Leaders

Effective leaders use negotiation strategies that reflect their style, goals, and context. Here are some examples:

❖ Building Trust and Rapport: Leaders who establish trust and rapport with others are more likely to succeed in negotiation. They do this by listening actively, acknowledging others' concerns, and finding common ground.

❖ Setting Clear Goals and Priorities: Leaders who define their goals and priorities before negotiation are better equipped to negotiate effectively. They do this by anticipating challenges, identifying interests and needs, and developing a negotiation strategy.

❖   Using Power and Influence Wisely: Leaders who use their power and influence wisely can achieve their goals without alienating others. They do this by balancing assertiveness and flexibility, using persuasion and framing, and avoiding coercion or manipulation.

❖   Empowering Others: Leaders who empower others in negotiation can foster collaboration and creativity. They do this by delegating authority, encouraging participation, and sharing credit and rewards.

❖   Leading Cross-Cultural Negotiations: Leaders who lead cross-cultural negotiations need to adapt their style and strategies to the cultural norms and values of others. They do this by understanding communication styles, avoiding stereotypes and biases, and showing respect and openness.

❖   Overcoming Leadership Challenges: Leaders who face challenges in negotiation, such as limited authority, conflicting goals, or difficult personalities, need to be creative and resilient. They do this by seeking common ground, building coalitions, or using third-party assistance.

Leadership Challenges in Negotiation

Leadership challenges can arise in negotiation when leaders face complex or contentious issues, deal with multiple stakeholders, or confront ethical dilemmas. Here are some examples:

❖   Balancing Conflicting Interests: Leaders who negotiate with multiple parties with conflicting interests need to balance their own goals with the needs of others. They may face pressure to compromise or sacrifice their own interests for the common good.

❖   Dealing with Limited Authority: Leaders who negotiate

without full authority from their organization need to be creative and persuasive to achieve their goals. They may need to seek approval or support from others or leverage their personal power and influence.

❖ Maintaining Ethical Standards: Leaders who negotiate in situations where ethical or legal standards are at risk need to balance their responsibilities as negotiators and leaders. They may need to disclose information, reject unfair or illegal offers, or resign from negotiations if necessary.

❖ Coping with Personality Conflicts: Leaders who negotiate with difficult personalities, such as aggressive, passive, emotional, or analytical negotiators, need to adjust their style and strategies to match the situation. They may need to build rapport, use effective communication, or take a pause to defuse tensions.

Conclusion

Negotiation and leadership are complementary skills that require preparation, communication, creativity, and empathy. Effective leaders know how to negotiate skilfully to achieve their goals while building trust, collaboration, and long-term relationships with others. They also know how to overcome challenges and adapt to different contexts and cultures. As negotiation becomes more complex and global, leaders need to continue learning and improving their negotiation skills to stay competitive and make a positive impact on their organizations and the world.

CHAPTER 20: CONCLUSION AND FUTURE OF NEGOTIATION

Negotiation is a vital skill that we use every day, not just in business but also in our personal lives. As we explored in this book, negotiation is an art that takes time and practice to master. We discussed the fundamentals of negotiation, the importance of communication, the creation of value, and dealing with conflict. We also explored the impact of culture and personality on negotiation, and the importance of ethics in the negotiation process.

As we look to the future of negotiation, we can see the impact of technology on the negotiation process. We live in a world where negotiations can take place online, with the use of video conferencing and other digital tools. The rise of artificial intelligence (AI) is also changing the negotiation landscape. For example, AI technology can help reduce cultural misunderstandings by providing real-time language translation tools.

Another trend we can see in the future of negotiation is the rise of virtual reality. Negotiators will be able to create virtual environments for negotiations, which can help remove the barriers of distance and cultural differences. This technology might also help create more empathy and understanding between the parties.

The importance of lifelong learning in negotiation cannot be overstated. As new technologies and trends emerge, it is crucial to stay updated on the latest techniques and strategies. The negotiation landscape is always changing, and we need to adapt to these changes to stay competitive.

Finally, negotiation can play a vital role in creating a better world. The ability to negotiate fairly and ethically can help resolve conflicts and promote cooperation. As we continue to face global challenges, from climate change to economic inequality, we need effective negotiation skills more than ever.

Negotiation is an art, and like any art, it takes time and practice to master. By understanding the fundamentals of negotiation, we can create value, deal with conflict, and build strong relationships. As we look to the future, we can see the impact of technology on the negotiation process, and the importance of ongoing learning and adaptation. By using negotiation effectively, we can help build a better world for ourselves and future generations.

Final Thoughts

The art of negotiation is a skill that can be honed and improved upon with practice, experience, and a willingness to learn. It is not a one-size-fits-all approach but rather requires adaptability and understanding of the specific situation at hand.

Negotiation is not about winning or losing but rather finding a mutually beneficial solution. It's about building relationships and creating opportunities for long-lasting partnerships.

As we have explored in this book, negotiation involves preparation, active listening, clear communication, and the ability to remain calm under pressure. It also requires empathy and the ability to put oneself in the other party's shoes.

Remember that every negotiation presents an opportunity for growth and learning. Don't let fear or pride get in the way of reaching a successful outcome.

I hope this book has provided you with valuable insights into the art of negotiation. Whether you are negotiating in business or personal matters, may you approach each situation with confidence, grace, and an open mind. Here's to successful negotiations and meaningful connections!

ABOUT THE AUTHOR

Ray Goodwin

Ray Goodwin, is the author behind this series of captivating books on Business Development and self improvement, and has left an indelible mark on the field. He was born and raised in the bustling city of London, where he developed a strong work ethic and an insatiable curiosity about the inner workings of successful businesses. Throughout his illustrious career, Ray leveraged his extensive knowledge and experience to help numerous companies flourish and prosper.

His keen insights and innovative strategies has earned him recognition, driving him to share his expertise with others. Ray believes in the power of sharing knowledge to elevate businesses and empower aspiring entrepreneurs.

Ray's dedication to his craft is evident in the numerous books he has authored on business development and self improvement. His writing style seamlessly blends practical advice, thought-provoking concepts, and real-life case studies, making his books invaluable resources for business professionals and novices alike. His ability to distill complex concepts into accessible language has greatly impacted the lives and careers of countless individuals.

Now retired from the corporate world, Ray and his beloved wife have settled in the idyllic English countryside. Surrounded by the beauty of nature, Ray finds inspiration for his writing and indulges in his hobbies.

Ray Goodwin's books continue to serve as enduring guides for those seeking success in the business world. With a wealth of experience and a deep understanding of the inner workings of businesses, Ray's work remains a testament to his passion for sharing knowledge and helping others flourish.